For Josiah, Nyah, Eboni and Imari

<u>Things I Wish I Knew, When I Was Young Like You</u>

Written by: Moses Miller
Edited by: Eboni Symone Porter
Illustrated by: Kathy Garren

Text Copyright 2012 Moses Miller
Illustrations Copyright 2012 Kathy Garren

ISBN 10: 0-9786929-5-0
ISBN 13: 978-0-9786929-5-7
LCCN: 2012934292

Published by: Mind Candy, LLC.
www.MindCandyMedia.com

It is often said, that the youth of today have very little respect for the knowledge and wisdom that comes from the older generation...

...so, sometimes it's better for them to learn life lessons from one of their peers.

IT'S OKAY TO CRY

It's only natural to show emotions. I remember falling from the top of a twenty-foot slide one day and landing hard on my stomach, when I was in elementary school. I was in a lot of pain, but I refused to cry. I was always told that boys don't cry. Boys had to be tough. If a boy cried, he was acting like a girl. So that day, I didn't let anyone see me shed a tear.

But, everyone gets sad at times. In life, there will be moments when you will also experience pain. It's not healthy to hold on to those feelings. Most bullies are really in pain. Even if they have a smile on their face, they are hurting inside. However, instead of dealing with their own problems, they take their pain out on others. People who are hurting, hurt others.

CONFESSIONS OF A BULLY

Some say that I am evil, but that simply is not true,
My heart is filled with tons of pain, that I take out on you
So, I pick and I tease, I fight and I yell,
Hiding my true feelings, behind a hardened shell
To make people like me, I often will use fear,
Afraid to be honest or even be sincere
Because if you knew the truth, then surely you would see,
The problem's not with you, the problem is with me
No one knows my pain, or understands me fully,
I just want to be loved, but I choose to play bully

Written by: The School Bully

LET'S TALK ABOUT IT

1. WHAT IS THE DEFINITION OF A BULLY?
2. WHY DO SOME KIDS BECOME BULLIES?
3. IN WHAT WAYS DO BULLIES HURT OTHER PEOPLE'S LIVES?
4. WHAT SHOULD YOU DO IF YOU ARE BEING BULLIED BY SOMEONE?
5. WHY IS IT IMPORTANT TO LET SOMEONE KNOW WHEN YOU ARE IN PAIN?
6. WHY ARE SOME CHILDREN AFRAID TO TELL THEIR PARENTS THEY ARE BEING BULLIED?
7. HOW CAN BEING BULLIED MAKE SOMEONE FEEL ABOUT THEMSELVES?
8. CAN GIRLS BE BULLIES TOO?
9. HOW SHOULD BULLIES BE TREATED?
10. CAN BULLIES CHANGE?

STARS ARE STRANGERS TOO...

Ever since I was little, I was always told to stay away from strangers. My parents would say, "Don't talk to strangers, they may hurt you!" When I was in first grade, a strange man tried to kidnap me. Fortunately, my mother saw him and was able to scare him away before he took me.

There are many strangers who prey on young children like you and wish to do them harm. Some may approach children at the park or outside of their school. Nowadays, others have even started using the internet as well. An adult should not try to have a relationship with a child without the permission of their parents. So, not only should you avoid talking to strangers, you should not listen to them either.

Did you know that some stars are strangers too? Just because they're on television and they are famous, it doesn't mean that we should listen to them or follow everything they say or what we see them do. Some stars are positive role models, while some aren't very good people at all.

Just like a stranger, we don't know them, so we should be very careful when it comes to being like certain stars. Some stars commit crimes, go to jail, have violent fights, do drugs and other bad things as well. Just because they're on television, in magazines or act in movie roles, it doesn't mean we should try to be like them.

STARS ARE STRANGERS TOO...

MY ROLE MODEL IS NOT...

MY ROLE MODEL IS NOT A CHEATER, A LIAR, A THUG
OR A THIEF,
MY ROLE MODEL IS NOT SOMEONE WHO JOINS GANGS
OR HANGS OUT ON THE STREET
MY ROLE MODEL IS NOT A DRUG DEALER OR A DRUG USER,
MY ROLE MODEL IS NOT SOMEONE WHO HITS FEMALES
OR A CHILD ABUSER
MY ROLE MODEL IS NOT A DEADBEAT DAD
OR A DEADBEAT MOM,
MY ROLE MODEL IS NOT SOMEONE WHO COMMITS CRIMES
OR GOES TO JAIL LIKE A CON
MY ROLE MODEL IS RESPONSIBLE, KIND, TRUSTWORTHY
AND TRUE,
MY ROLE MODEL SAYS THE RIGHT THINGS
AND DOES THE RIGHT THINGS TOO

JUL   Issue Number 207

The Daily Star

Popular Teen Idol Arrested on Drug Charges

Ready For Rehab?

Movie Star set to get the help he desperately needs

Page 14

Too fast and too furious ...

Rap star charged with assaulting female fan

Page 21

LET'S TALK ABOUT IT

1. WHAT IS A ROLE MODEL TO YOU?
2. WHO ARE SOME OF YOUR ROLE MODELS?
3. IS SOMEONE A ROLE MODEL JUST BECAUSE YOU SEE THEM ON TELEVISION OR IN MUSIC VIDEOS?
4. CAN SOMEONE'S BEHAVIOR MAKE THEM NO LONGER BE SEEN AS A GOOD ROLE MODEL BY OTHERS?
5. WHY DO SOME KIDS LOOK AT DRUG DEALERS, GANG MEMBERS AND OTHER CRIMINALS AS ROLE MODELS?
6. CAN PARENTS OR SIBLINGS BE CONSIDERED ROLE MODELS?
7. CAN PARENTS OR SIBLINGS BE BAD ROLE MODELS?
8. HOW CAN YOU BE A POSITIVE ROLE MODEL?

LIFE IS NOT A VIDEOGAME

In most videogames, the objective is to shoot, kill, harm or hurt others in order to get to the next stage, complete the level or win the game. If you die, you get another life, so you can go back to killing again. You don't get rewarded for good behavior or being compassionate towards others. Instead, you are encouraged to be as cruel as possible, hurting others so you can win.

That is not what life is all about. Caring people don't hurt others, just so they can get ahead. Caring people treat others like they would want to be treated. We should be kind to other children like our classmates and never tease or bully anyone, because we wouldn't want to be bullied ourselves.

In videogames, you get another life if you make a mistake. Unfortunately, in real life we have to deal with the consequences of our actions. In videogames, you get rewarded for hurting others. In real life, you get punished.

We don't always get rewarded in real life for being kind or nice. However, that does not give us the right to be mean or hurtful to other people. We should be kind to others because it's the right thing to do. Kind and compassionate people care about how their actions make others feel.

JUST BECAUSE

Terry grew up in the apartment buildings on a street named Terrace Avenue. Some people call them projects, but he just called them buildings. His neighborhood wasn't the best, but his mother always said, "Even if the place where you come from isn't the very best, you should always do your very best." I guess that's why he studied hard and did well in school. He knew if he did his best, he would have a chance to do better for himself and his family in the future.

A lot of elderly people lived in his building. The elevators were broken quite often, and they'd have to take the steps up to their apartments. Terry would feel sorry for them, because walking up the steps was hard enough, and oftentimes they would have to carry their own groceries all the way up to their apartments as well.

Even though there were always young people in the lobby, they never extended a hand to help. They were too busy to care about anybody other than themselves. However, whenever Terry was around he would carry their bags up to their apartments for them.

One cold winter day, Terry helped his elderly neighbor, Ms. Baker bring her groceries up to her apartment. She had a grandson his age, but he didn't help her much.

Shortly after they walked up to Ms. Baker's apartment, she asked Terry, "Why do you always help the old people like me with their groceries?"

"Just because," he replied.

"Just because, huh?" she asked.

"Yeah, just because," he repeated.

Terry didn't have much more to say. To him it was only right to help those in need. He never wanted anything in return. He just hoped that someday if he ever needed a helping hand, someone would do the same for him. He knew that we all need help at times. None of us can get through life all alone.

Years later, Terry went off to college on an academic scholarship he received for doing very good in school. He pursued a degree in Social Work, because he wanted to help young people who needed assistance in his community.

When Terry finished college, he got a job working at a community center just a few blocks from where he once lived. Two weeks after starting his new job, he received a letter in the mail from a lawyer. After opening the envelope, he immediately became sad. The letter said that Ms. Baker had passed away.

One thing about the elderly is that they often sacrifice by working hard when they're younger, just so they can provide for their families. And unfortunately, when they get older and are in need themselves, younger people tend to forget about the sacrifices they once made.

Terry was blessed with the chance to speak with Ms. Baker many times over the years and she taught him a lot. Older people are wise and they have so much to share. If more people took the time to talk to them, they would be surprised at how much they could learn.

There was also something else inside the envelope Terry received. It was a check made out in his name. Apparently, Ms. Baker had written him into her will before she died. The check that she left for him was written out for one-hundred-thousand dollars. Attatched to the check was a small note that simply said the words, "Just Because."

LET'S TALK ABOUT IT

1. DO YOU KNOW ANYONE WHO PLAYS VIOLENT VIDEOGAMES?
2. WHY DO THEY PLAY THESE GAMES?
3. DO YOU THINK THAT PLAYING VIOLENT VIDEOGAMES CAN MAKE SOMEONE ACT VIOLENTLY?
4. WHY DO YOUNG PEOPLE TREAT THE ELDERLY MEAN AT TIMES AND SHOW THEM NO RESPECT?
5. WHAT WOULD YOUR FRIENDS SAY IF THEY SAW YOU HELPING OUT AN ELDERLY PERSON?
6. WHAT GOOD DEEDS DO YOU DO TO HELP OTHERS?

WE'RE ALL DIFFERENT BUT THE SAME

One of the first friends I had, did not have skin the same color as mine. It didn't matter to me and it didn't matter to him much either. He liked to play tag and videogames just like me, and we both loved going to gym class. We hated math, but in art we always found time to talk and draw characters from our favorite television shows. We were the best of friends.

The beauty of us all is that we are all different. We all come in different shapes, sizes and colors, which makes us all beautiful in our own unique ways. However, we are all very much the same. We each have the need to be loved, to feel appreciated and to have a sense of security.

By meeting and becoming friends with people outside of your own race, you will learn a lot about other cultures. This world is a giant melting pot, made up of people who come from many different races, backgrounds and beliefs. By getting to know one another better, we can avoid many misunderstandings that can lead to other problems. As you get to know more people, it won't be long before you realize that we really are all different, but the same.

JUST LIKE YOU AND ME

Felicia told me that the new girl in our class is poor. She must be because it's only her third day in our school and she has already worn the same pair of pants twice. The shirts she wears are not name brand like the rest of ours and they all look old and dirty. Dawn calls her "Broke Belinda" behind her back, even though she smiles in her face. Dawn is the most popular girl in our class and she always has something mean to say, just to get people to laugh at others.

The new girl is Hispanic, and Felecia doesn't hang out with the Spanish girls because they're different. They don't dress or speak like us and they surely don't act like us either. They're just different and that's why we stay apart from one another.

Today, our teacher Ms. Thompson assigned our seats during our bus trip to the museum. Felecia was looking forward to the trip since the beginning of the school year, and now here it was. As luck would have it, she was forced to sit next to "Broke Belinda." Every chance I got, I glanced toward the back of the bus where Felicia was sitting. I could tell she wasn't having much fun.

It took her and Belinda a long time to talk. Finally, Belinda broke the ice by asking, "Have you been to the museum before?" She spoke with an accent.

Felicia told her she had. Actually, she'd been there two other times last year and the year before. Belinda explained that she had never seen a museum. Her home country was El Salvador, before she traveled up north with her mother and her two sisters. They used the little money they saved to make it to the United States. She was young, but she had seen wars and many other things Felicia couldn't even imagine.

All she ever wanted was a safe place to live and an education just like we had growing up. She shared clothes with her younger sister, but she never complained. She didn't judge people by how much money they had or the name brands on their clothes and she hoped that people treated her the same way.

When lunch time arrived, the two girls shared the food they had packed and continued to exchange stories with one another. On the bus trip back to school, Ms. Thompson allowed us to sit anywhere we wanted, but the two girls decided not to change their seats. Before the bus pulled out of the parking lot at the musuem, Dawn walked up to Felicia and whispered, "You're gonna sit with Broke Belinda agan?"

Felicia looked her in the eyes and said, "Her name is just, Belinda and she's my friend."

Dawn walked off after sucking her teeth, while Felicia and Belinda picked up talking where they had left off.

Unlike Dawn, Belinda didn't talk bad about people. That was one of the many things that Felicia liked about her. She also liked the fact that she was compassionate and kind. I guess it's true when they say, we're all different, but the same.

I asked Felicia if the new girl was different and she said, "She's just like you and me."

LET'S TALK ABOUT IT

1. DO YOU HAVE FRIENDS WHO ARE ORIGINALLY FROM A DIFFERENT COUNTRY THAN YOU?

2. IF SO, WHAT DO YOU NOTICE IS THE SAME AND WHAT DIFFERENCES DO YOU HAVE?

3. WHY DO SOME CHILDREN SEPARATE THEMSELVES FROM CHILDREN OF DIFFERENT CULTURES?

4. WHAT ARE SOME OF THE CHALLENGES CHILDREN FACE WHEN THEY COME TO AMERICA FROM ANOTHER COUNTRY?

5. DO YOU KNOW WHAT THE WORD RACISM MEANS?

6. WHAT DID FELICIA SHOW BY CHOOSING TO SIT NEXT TO BELINDA?

7. IS IT OKAY TO SAY BAD THINGS ABOUT PEOPLE BEHIND THEIR BACKS?

FEAR PRESSURE

A friend wouldn't hurt you. A friend wouldn't try to get a friend to do bad things. A friend wouldn't ask you to cheat, lie, steal or do anything that could get you into trouble. If a friend tries to convince you to do bad things, then they really aren't one of your friends.

Some people will try to pressure you into doing bad things by using peer pressure. Peer pressure is when someone or a group of people try to convince you to behave like them, whether it's good or bad. I call it "fear pressure," because people who give in are usually afraid to be different than everybody else. Don't ever be afraid to be different from people who are doing bad things.

People in gangs do bad things. Even though they may try to get you to join them and be a part of their "family", they are not your friends. You don't want any parts of that kind of family. Friends wouldn't try to convince you to be a part of anything that could result in you getting hurt, put in prison or possibly even killed.

WHAT ABOUT YOUR FRIENDS?

Joell grew up in a single family household with his mother and his younger sister, Maritza who was four-years-old. Joell was only eight, but he already felt very much alone. Even though his mother cared for him and constantly spoiled him by buying the best sneakers and the latest videogames, often-times he felt sad. He missed his father and didn't understand why he didn't want to be a part of his life. Without an answer, Joell blamed himself.

When his mother showed Maritza attention, it made him jealous and mad. To deal with his anger, he would tease his sister when his mother wasn't around. While he was at school, he would also pick on other children and act disrespectful towards his teachers. He liked being the class clown because it got him attention, but he still wasn't happy with himself.

When Joell turned nine, a bad group of older boys asked him to join their gang. They had heard about his reputation and knew that he would do anything to fit in with them. One day Joell's new group of "friends" thought that it would be a good idea to steal from a local grocery store. Joell waited outside as a lookout while the rest of his boys went in the store. He knew he shouldn't be there, but he wanted to fit in.

A few minutes later, the boys ran out of the store with their hands filled with candy and chips. Joell ran off chasing behind them. When they reached a park a few blocks away, they stopped to eat all of the goodies they had just stolen.

Unknown to them, was the fact that the owner of the store had called the police. Before they could finish enjoying the snacks they had stolen, the police were at the park arresting the boys. Joell didn't actually steal anything himself, but because he was with the group who did, he was treated the same.

When his mother arrived at the police precinct to pick him up, she was very sad.

She worked two jobs and used her hard earned money to buy Joell anything he ever wanted, so he didn't need to steal. Now she had to face the embarrassment of picking her son up from a police station.

It didn't make Joell feel good to see his mother sad. Doing bad things didn't make him feel any better about himself. Now he had a bad reputation, a group of "friends" who only liked him because he got into trouble like them and a mother who was deeply hurt.

When Joell got home, he sat in his room and wondered what to do next? How could he make everything better? He knew it wasn't in his best interest to continue to do bad things, but he was confused. The people he would hang around with always encouraged him to get in trouble. What about your friends?

LET'S TALK ABOUT IT

1. WHAT WOULD YOUR ADVICE TO JOELL BE?
2. WOULD A FRIEND EVER TELL YOU TO DO SOMETHING BAD?
3. WHO ARE SOME OF THE PEOPLE JOELL SHOULD SPEAK TO ABOUT THE WAY HE IS FEELING?
4. DO YOU KNOW ANYONE LIKE JOELL?
5. WHY WOULD SOMEONE WHO DOESN'T NEED TO STEAL TAKE SOMETHING THAT DOESN'T BELONG TO THEM?
6. CAN THE BAD THINGS YOU DO HURT YOUR PARENTS?
7. WHY WOULD SOMEONE WHO IS SPOILED WITH THE LATEST VIDEOGAMES AND TOYS STILL FEEL SAD AND EMPTY INSIDE?
8. HOW CAN YOU SAY "NO," TO A PERSON WHO WANTS YOU TO DO BAD THINGS WITH THEM?

APPRECIATE WHAT YOU HAVE

There's nothing wrong with wanting more than what you have. The reason many people work hard in school and at their jobs is so they can have better things and provide more for their families. However, we should always be thankful for what we have. We should never hurt others, just so we can get ahead.

So many people complain about the things that they want or don't have, instead of showing appreciation for their blessings. Each day, we should be grateful for just being alive and having good health, because there are so many people who aren't fortunate enough to have the things we take for granted.

THE POOR LITTLE RICH KID

When my brother, James was a child, he had a classmate named David, who everyone said was rich. His parents drove him to school everyday in nice luxury cars and once he was even dropped off in a limousine. He had the nicest clothes and always wore the latest sneakers. For most of the school year, everyone wished they could have the things that he had.

For my brother's birthday that year, one of my cousins gave him a hooded sweatshirt. It wasn't name-brand and it wasn't new. There was a little tear on the sleeve, but it was warm and he wore it proudly. He even got a few compliments from his classmates about it. Unfortunately, he only had the sweatshirt for two weeks, before he lost it. He left it in the playground and it wasn't there when he returned.

A little over a month later, my brother was at the park after school and he saw David playing with his friends. David acted strange when he saw James, and my brother immediately knew why.

David was wearing his sweatshirt. When James asked him about it, he denied that it belonged to him, even though it was torn on the sleeve at the same exact place.

When James got home later that day, he told my parents what happened. They told him not to worry because they would take care of it. More importantly, they wanted him to learn a valuable lesson. Sometimes we look at other people and want what they have. In David's case, it looked like he had everything in the world, but he wanted my brother's hand-me-down sweater. He wasn't grateful for all the things his parents did for him and gave to him daily.

For James, he was always happy even when he didn't have a lot. However, from then on, he learned to appreciate the little things even more. He shared with others and felt grateful when they shared with him. Everyday, he woke up grateful for at least one thing.

David's parents bought him a new sweater to replace the one he had taken, and he gave the stolen sweater back to my brother. He didn't apologize, but James heard him bragging to some of his classmates about his sweater being new and the sweater James had being old and dirty. He also told people that my parents couldn't afford to buy James a new sweater, but my brother ignored his insults.

Years later, James told me he was watching the news one night and he saw a story about a man with a familiar face. It was David. He had grown up and become a successful businessman, just like his father.

But sadly, he was arrested for stealing from some people who trusted him with their money. He was rich, but he still wanted more. Unfortunately, he never learned his lesson. I guess even as an adult he didn't appreciate what he had. Poor little rich kid.

LET'S TALK ABOUT IT

1. WHAT DOES "TREAT OTHERS LIKE YOU WANT TO BE TREATED," MEAN TO YOU?

2. WHY IS THE BOY IN THE PICTURE AT THE BEGINNING OF POOR LITTLE RICH KID UNHAPPY?

3. HOW CAN YOU SHOW YOUR PARENTS THAT YOU APPRECIATE THE THINGS YOU HAVE?

4. WHAT MAKES YOU HAPPY?

5. CAN YOU NAME ONE THING YOU APPRECIATE?

6. CAN YOU BUY HAPPINESS?

Most people know a clown when they see one. They usually have make-up on their faces, a funny outfit and a colorful wig on their head. You can also spot a policeman or a fireman quite easily as well by the uniform that they wear.

You would never mistake a fireman for a clown or a policeman for a fireman. They all dress a certain way so people can easily identify who they are. Believe it or not, every day you wear a uniform as well. The way you dress says a lot about you.

Before you even open your mouth, people are judging you by your appearance. Whether it is right or wrong, it is true. You have probably done it yourself before. It's human nature.

That is why it's very important that you wear clothes that are appropriate for your age. When young girls try to dress and look older than they are, it can be very dangerous for them. Unfortunately, there are bad people in this world who prey on young females. The way they dress can draw the attention of these bad individuals.

For young boys, it is just as important that they wear the appropriate "uniform" each day. Bad people also prey on boys, wanting to do them nothing but harm. Gangs often look to recruit new members who look, dress and act like them. In many people's eyes, you are only what they see. Make sure you do your best to always show the world who you really are.

THE BOY WHO PLAYED WOLF

Instead of being a child, learning and focusing on the things that someone his age should, ten-year-old Jeremiah had other things on his mind. At one time he was a good student, but recently he stopped trying his best in class. After school he watched music videos, played violent videogames and enjoyed the crime shows on television about the gang lifestyle. Before long, he knew how to make gang signs, knew the colors they wore and even started to dress as they did.

One day, Jeremiah was walking home with his pants hanging low so his underwear could be seen and he had a bandana tied around his neck. He had changed the way he dressed without his parents knowing, adjusting his pants and putting the scarf around his neck each morning before he got to school.

He was only a few blocks from his house when a group of teenagers walked up to him. They noticed how he was dressed and the way he carried himself,

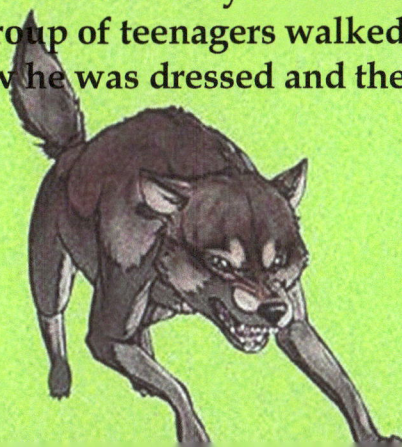

and thought that he may be a member of a rival gang. Jeremiah denied that he was in a gang, but they didn't believe him no matter what he said. Before he knew it, he was completely surrounded with nowhere to go.

There were several people looking out of their windows watching everything as it took place. They knew that the young boy didn't have a chance against the large group. However, they also looked at how the boy was dressed. He had his pants hanging down low and his appearance was just like the other boys.

Instead of helping or even calling the police, they just watched from afar. None of them knew him personally. They figured he was just like the rest of the group and was up to no good. They believed that he probably deserved what was about to happen.

Jeremiah looked like them, he dressed like them and he acted like them as well. If they thought he was one of the "good kids," someone would have probably come to his aid. But, instead they judged him by how he looked, like most people do. The boy who played wolf.

LET'S TALK ABOUT IT

1. IS THE WAY YOU DRESS IMPORTANT? WHY?
2. DO YOU BELIEVE THAT PEOPLE JUDGE YOU BY THE WAY YOU LOOK AND ACT?
3. DO YOU THINK IT IS FAIR FOR PEOPLE TO JUDGE YOU BY YOUR APPEARANCE?
4. DO YOU KNOW ANYONE IN A GANG?
5. IS IT BETTER TO TRY TO ACT LIKE EVERYONE ELSE JUST TO FIT IN WITH A GROUP, OR TO JUST BE YOURSELF?
6. HOW DO YOU THINK JEREMIAH'S STORY ENDS?

Adults have a responsibility to pass on their knowledge, wisdom and understanding too...

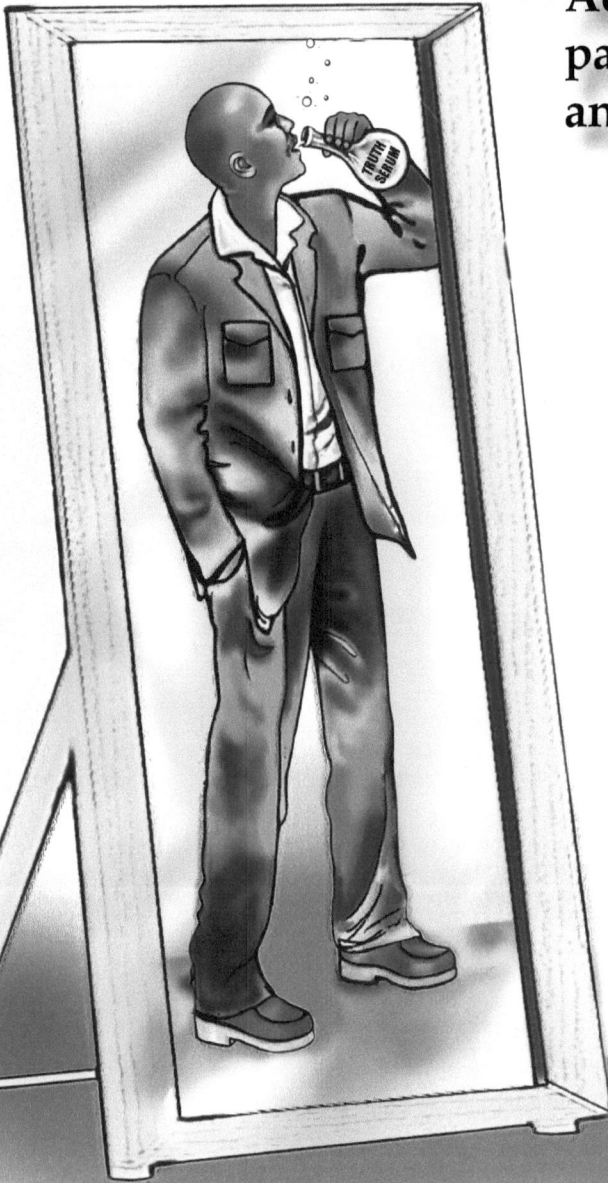

...that's why I shared these things I wish I knew, when I was young like you.

Author Moses Miller

I wrote THINGS I WISH I KNEW, WHEN I WAS YOUNG LIKE YOU because I know how important it is for you to make good decisions at a young age. Throughout your life, you will be faced with a lot of tough challenges. You will also have to cope with peer pressure from "friends" who may try to convince you to do bad things that are not in your best interest. You need to think ahead, before you act and make sure you know what the results of your actions may be. If you're fortunate, you have adults in your life who will attempt to offer you good advice. Please take the time to listen. Like me, they only want the best for you. I hope you enjoyed this book. And I also wish you the very best that life can offer.

Sincerely,

Mr. Moses Miller

Moses Miller is a journalist, motivational speaker and an award winning author who captures the pulse of the streets with intelligent and well thought out storylines. As a socially conscious individual, Mr. Miller has played a key role in helping to improve the literacy rates amongst African American and Hispanic youth. Mr. Miller's inspirational book **The Barack in Me**, was written specifically for young African American males, with themes that cross the boundaries of gender and race. Currently, Mr. Miller is the facilitator for four youth mentoring programs focused on developing upstanding young men and community leaders.

www.MindCandyMedia.com
Email: Moses@MindCandyMedia.com
Facebook: www.Facebook.com/AuthorMosesMiller
Twitter: Twitter.com/MosesMiller

DEDICATIONS

This book is dedicated to Lindsay Volpe, Zachary Knight-Ward, Victor Garrison, Jr, Zion Fenner, Jizzixious Bishop, Joseph Torres, Andy Cuba, Tyrone Garza, Jr, and the countless young men I have had the pleasure to work with and mentor over the years. I value the relationships and bonds we have formed and look forward to watching each and every one of you continue your successful journeys through life, as you strive to reach your full potential.

Always chase your dreams. Always pursue your goals. Always do your best. And always do what's right.

Your friend and your supporter,

Mr. Moses Miller

love, kindness, compassion, humility, appreciation, responsibility, loyalty, honesty, patience, attitude, preparation, perseverance, respect, integrity, courage, self-control, empathy, sympathy, gratitude, tolerance, duty, love, kindness, compassion, humility, appreciation, responsibility, loyalty, honesty, patience, attitude, preparation, perseverance, respect, integrity, courage, self-control, empathy, sympathy, gratitude, tolerance, duty, love, kindness, compassion, humility, appreciation, responsibility, loyalty, honesty, patience ,attitude, preparation, perseverance, respect, integrity, courage, self-control, empathy, sympathy, gratitude, tolerance, duty, love, kindness, compassion, humility, appreciation, responsibility, loyalty, honesty, patience, attitude, preparation, perseverance, respect, integrity, courage, self-control, empathy, sympathy, gratitude, tolerance, duty, love, kindness, compassion, humility, appreciation, responsibility, loyalty, honesty, patience, attitude, preparation, perseverance, respect, integrity, courage, self-control, empathy, sympathy, gratitude, tolerance, duty, love, kindness, compassion, humility, appreciation, responsibility, loyalty, honesty, patience, attitude, preparation, perseverance, respect, integrity, courage, self-control, empathy, sympathy, gratitude, tolerance, duty, love, kindness, compassion, humility, appreciation, responsibility, loyalty, honesty, patience, attitude, preparation, perseverance, respect, integrity, courage, self-control, empathy, sympathy, gratitude, tolerance, duty, love, kindness, compassion, humility, appreciation, responsibility, loyalty, honesty, patience, attitude, preparation, perseverance, respect, integrity, courage, self-control, empathy, sympathy, gratitude, tolerance, duty, love, kindness, compassion, humility, appreciation, responsibility, loyalty, honesty, patience, attitude, preparation, perseverance, respect, integrity, courage, self-control, empathy, sympathy, gratitude, tolerance, duty, love, kindness, compassion, humility, appreciation, responsibility, loyalty, honesty, patience, attitude, preparation, perseverance, respect, integrity, courage, self-control, empathy, sympathy, gratitude, tolerance, duty, love, kindness, compassion, humility, appreciation, responsibility, loyalty, honesty, patience, attitude, preparation, perseverance, respect, integrity, courage, self-control, empathy, sympathy, gratitude, tolerance, duty

www.ingramcontent.com/pod-product-compliance
Lightning Source LLC
LaVergne TN
LVHW072119070426
835511LV00002B/26